[i]INTERNATIONAL TRADE- IMPORTING/EXPORTING: BECOMING A LICENSED CUSTOMS BROKER

Table of Contents:

2. CUSTOMS BROKER EXAMINATION TRAINING AND DEVELOPMENT PROGRAM FOR ENTREPRENEURS AND SMALL BUSINESSES. www.cctradeimports.com http://customsbroker.eventbrite.com

3. THE CUSTOMS AND TRADE AUTOMATED INTERFACE REQUIREMENTS (CATAIR) see www.cbp.gov for downloadable document.

4. TARIFF SCHEDULE Chapter Headings. Downloadable document and purchased at the Government Book Store.

LICENSED CUSTOMS BROKERS

About the Profession:

Customs brokering is a profession that is detailed oriented and specialized, its description has undergone several changes. It has evolved to a well-structured respectable profession. Today, the US Customs and Border Protection (CBP) controls and regulates all activities regarding customs business.

A Customs Broker is a person, association or firm licensed and regulated by CBP agency to assist importers and exporters and to perform customs transactions on their behalf. Customs brokers submit necessary documents, make payments on the behalf of their clients and charge them a fee for these services.

Brokers must have necessary knowledge and experience regarding the procedures, valuations, classification, requirements, regulations, accounting, taxes and fees for import and export of merchandise.

According to the US Customs and Border Protection Agency (CBP), the are approximately 11,000 active Customs Brokers in the United States.

To become a Customs Broker, you need to get a license except for a few exceptional conditions listed below:

1. If a person is involved in the business of entry, clearance or regulation of vessels as per navigation laws, he doesn't require a broker's license.

2. A carrier involved in arrival or clearance

of merchandise is permitted to make entries for that merchandise without being a licensed broker.

3. A person, provided he meets the requirements of 19 CFR § 141.33, is not required to have a broker's license.

4. A foreign trade zone user does not need a broker's license as long as his activities are in a zone that is not part of the United States Customs territory.

5. An importer or exporter, involved in his own customs business transactions, does not need a license for himself or his employees.

6. An employee of the broker who works

only for his employer's interest does not require a license when:

6.A)   The employee is authorized by the broker to sign customs business related documents on his behalf and has the power of attorney for the same.

6.B)   The broker has submitted a statement to the Director of the Port stating that the employee is authorized to perform transactions on his behalf. A statement is not necessary when the broker is operating under an exception to the district permit rule.

Procedure to obtain Customs Broker's License:

Let us have a look at the eligibility criteria an individual needs to satisfy to become a Customs broker:

1. You should be a citizen of the United States of America and minimum 21 years of age.

2. You should not be an active employee of the Federal Government.

3. You should have a good moral character.

If you satisfy the eligibility criteria, you have to fulfill the following conditions:

1. You must pass the Customs Broker License Examination.

2. You have to submit an application to obtain the broker's license to CBP together with the required fees.

3. Your application has to be approved by CBP.

You need to submit your application on CBP Form 3124 in duplicate to the director of the port where you wish to do business. Along with the application, you need to pay $200 as application fee. The application should be submitted within three years of passing the written exam (with 75% and above).

About the Written Exam:

The written exam is four hours long and is an open book/open test with 80 multiple choice questions based on policies and procedures. Customs broker's license is proctored by CBP and its Headquarters is in Washington D.C . And the exams are released from there. The exam is generally conducted on the first Monday of April and October with the exception of a religious holiday then the exam with be giving on the following Tuesday. If you wish to take the exam, you need to inform the port director in writing at least 30 days before the day of exam and pay the $200 fee at that time. The port director will inform you of the date and time of the exam.

If you fail the exam, you are not eligible to submit your application for customs broker's license. However, you are allowed to appear for the exam again as per provisions of 19 CFR 111.13(b).

Appeal on failing the exam:

If you fail the exam, you are allowed to challenge the result by appealing to Trade Programs, Office of Field Operations within 60 days of the declaration of the result.

Authorization for Special Exam:

If an association or corporation loses the member with the customs broker's license before the next scheduled exam, CBP can authorize a special exam for an applicant from the company so that he can function as the licensed member. CBP can use its discretion to authorize a special written exam in some other conditions as well. For instance, if you as an individual want to continue your business as a sole proprietorship broker, you can request CBP to conduct a special exam for you.

You have to submit a request describing the conditions that require you to take the examination to the port director. If your request is accepted, the port director will inform you of the exact date, time and place of the exam. If you manage to pass the exam, you can go ahead and submit your application for the license. However, in case of a special exam you have to pay for the extra cost that CBP will incur to prepare and conduct the exam.

License:

After you pass the examination, you are eligible

to apply for the license:

The review of the application involves 3 stages.

1. Firstly, various agencies investigate your background. The investigation establishes the accuracy of your statements in the application, your business integrity and your character and reputation.

2. Next, the CBP port director goes through your original application and other details. He, then, forwards your application and the investigation report together with a recommendation to CBP Headquarters in Washington D.C.

3. The CBP will review the application and the Assistant Commissioner, Office of International Trade, will grant the license if he is satisfied with the application. You may be required to appear in person before the Assistant Commissioner for

written or oral inquiry.

The port director reserves the right to reject an improperly filed application. In such a case, the application along with the fees is returned to the applicant. If you have been denied the license after review of your application, you can appeal for a second opportunity to present more facts or argument in support of your application. You must file the request with Assistant Commissioner within 60 days of receiving the denial.

If the Assistant Commissioner decides to deny license to your application, a notice of denial in writing will be issued to you and the director of port where the application was submitted.

Your application can be rejected due to many reasons. Some of them are:

1. Any reason that justifies revocation of your license as per provisions of § 111.53

2. Inability to meet requirement given in §
   111.11

3. Failure to establish your good character or
   business integrity.

4. Unfair business practices

If you have been denied a license, you can
reapply for it after fulfilling the conditions in §
111.13(f).

As an applicant, you are allowed to withdraw
your application at any point in time before the
license is issued to you. However, on withdrawal
you will not be refunded the application fees of
$200.

If you wish to form a customs broker's
partnership, at least one of the partners should
have a broker's license.

For an association to be eligible for a broker's
license, it must:

1. Have the power under the clauses of association to perform customs business transactions as a broker.

2. Have at least one officer who is a licensed broker.

The license is issued to a particular individual and not in the name of his corporation or partnership.

Permit:

If you manage to successfully get the broker's license, you will also be issued a permit for the district in which the port you applied through is located. If proven to the port director that you are going to conduct your business only within that district and satisfy the conditions laid down in part 111, you will be exempted from paying $100 as fee for the permit. You need to have permit for the district where you wish to conduct your customs business. When you apply for a district permit, you should have a place and other arrangements in place to conduct your business.

However, if you wish to do customs business at ports in other districts or were not granted a permit with your license, you have to submit an application with the following documents to the port of director where you wish to do business:

1. Your broker's license number and it's date of issue

2. The address and telephone number of your office in that district

3. A copy of the document that mentions the registration of your business name with the local or state government

4. Name of the broker who will supervise and control the customs business transactions

5. The location where you intend to retain your brokerage records and the name of your recordkeeping contact

6. List of people that you will employ in that district along with specific information about the employees

Along with the application for national or district permit, you need to attach a number of documents and pay a permit fee of $100 and a user fee of $125. You have to pay $125 even when you get the permit concurrently with the license.

If you meet all the requirements, the port director will issue a district permit to you. However, if he feels that you should not be issued the permit, he has to submit his reasons for not granting you the required permit to the Office of Field Operations, CBP Headquarters.

Customs brokers with a district permit are

entitled to apply for a national permit. For this, they need to send an application to Office of Field Operations, CBP Headquarters.

Penalty:

A person found to be transacting customs business without a valid license is liable for penalty for all such individual transactions and other violations under the provision of 19 U.S.C 1641.

What about Customs Brokerages?

Corporations, partnerships, and associations must have a Broker's license to transact Customs Business. Each of these businesses must have at least one individually licensed officer, partner, or association to qualify the company's license. Failure to have a qualifying officer or member (of a partnership) for more than 120 days will result in the revocation of the Broker's license.

CC Imports, Inc. are licensed Customs Brokers specializing in the area of Intl Trade Training and Development Programs for Entrepreneurs, Small Businesses, Retirees, Business Professionals and Leaders. We have been in business since 2004, Our Intl Trade Coaches are all licensed Customs Brokers and are experienced Industry Leaders in International Trade. Currently, CC Imports, Inc. offers Intl Trade Training and Development Programs ranging from 2-Day Intl Trade Boot Camps, Intl Trade Workshops and 6 Month Training and Development which includes up to 4-15 minute sessions per month with an Intl Trade Coach. Want change in your business? Go global. Create opportunities in Intl Trade.

CUSTOMS BROKER TRAINING AND DEVELOPMENT PROGRAM FOR ENTREPRENEURS AND SMALL BUSINESSES.

CC Imports, Inc. provides International Trade Training and Development for Entrepreneurs, Leaders and Small Businesses. Our signature Intl Trade Empowerment Series is an intensive study and overview of US Customs Policies and Procedures covering customs directives and more. Our Training and Development Series are offered twice a year in the Spring and Fall usually six to eight weeks prior to the customs brokers licensing exam. Follow us on twitter.com/kcarrco and click "Like" on our Facebook page "INTERNATIONAL TRADE IMPORTS/EXPORTS, INTL TRADE CONSULTANT, CUSTOMS BROKER".

The examination that aspiring Customs Brokers have to appear for is designed to test your knowledge of laws, rules and regulations related to customs trade.

The US Customs Broker Examination Preparation Manual identifies several important subjects of Customs regulations that you, as a licensed customs broker, should know, in order to manage all responsibilities and activities involved in import clearance process.

Irrespective of your level of expertise in Customs regulations, the Manual is designed to give you maximum benefit. If you are preparing for the Customs broker examination, you should use the book for extensive studies. You can also carry this study aid to your examination room while appearing for the exam.

The book has 29 separate sections differentiated by tabs to make the reference easy during the exam. The book also contains questions from

Customs broker exams of previous years together with their answer keys. You can use these question papers to test your knowledge and to set an efficient tempo for the exam.

Here are some suggestions to research on website: www.cbp.gov:

1. Introduction to U.S. Customs and Border Protection (the General Basis & Legal Aspects)

2. General Aspects of Customs Brokerage

3. The Filing Identification Number

4. The Basic Importation Bond

5. The Entry Process

6. The Right to Make Entry

7. Customs Valuation & Tariff Classification

8. Customs Accounts, Bills and Duty Remittance

9. U.S. Rules of Origin

10. Country of Origin Marking Requirements

11. Import Quotas* Prior Disclosure

12. Liquidation of Entry

13. Examination, Detention and Release of Merchandise

14. Protests

15. Drawback

16. Supplemental Information Letters & Post Entry Amendments

17. Customs and Trade Automated Interface Requirements(CATAIR)/Automated

**THE CUSTOMS AND TRADE
AUTOMATED INTERFACE
REQUIREMENTS (CATAIR), downloadable
at www.cbp.gov.**

The CATAIR documents furnish information
regarding procedures required for importers or
their representatives to become Automated
Broker Interface (ABI) participants. The
documents also tell them how to supply
electronic import information to ABI and receive
information from it after they successfully
become a participant.

Currently, the ABI operates under the July 2004
version of CATAIR. However, ABI is dynamic
and thus, subject to change as and when new
enhancements and updates are added.

It is recommended that every active customs

broker should be acquainted with Automated Broker Interface (ABI) user interface. This interface is used by customs professionals as well as several members of the international trade community.

If you are a member of the international trade community and wish to participate in the Automated Broker Interface, you need to send a request along with some other information to the U.S Customs and Border Protection. For more detail regarding the documents you need to send check 19 CFR 143.2 (a) – (f).

After your letter is received by CBP, they will assign a Client Representative to help you with the process and to assist you in implementation of ABI in your company. You may also be subject to a background investigation aimed to verify your business integrity.

US TARIFF SCHEDULE is a downloadable document online and purchased in the Government Book Store.

There are different import regulations for various kinds of materials and it is important for a customs broker to be familiar with them. CC Imports, Inc. empowers Entrepreneurs and Small Businesses with an intensive study and overview of the Harmonized Tariff Schedule as Chapter and Section headings are given below:

SECTION I: Live Animals; Animal Products

SECTION II: Vegetable Products

SECTION III: Animal or Vegetable Fats and Oils and Their Cleavage Products; Prepared Edible Fats; Animal or Vegetable Waxes

SECTION IV: Prepared Foodstuffs; Beverages, Spirits, and Vinegar; Tobacco and Manufactured

Cellulosic Material; Waste and Scrap of Paper or Paperboard; Paper and Paperboard and Articles Thereof

SECTION XI: Textile and Textile Articles

SECTION XII: Footwear, Headgear, Umbrellas, Sun Umbrellas, Walking Sticks, Seat sticks, Whips, Riding-Crops and Parts Thereof; Prepared Feathers and Articles Made Therewith; Artificial Flowers; Articles Of Human Hair

SECTION XIII: Articles of Stone, Plaster, Cement, Asbestos, Mica or Similar Materials; Ceramic Products; Glass and Glassware

SECTION XIV: Natural Or Cultured Pearls, Precious Or Semiprecious Stones, Precious Metals, Metals Clad With Precious Metal, and Articles Thereof; Imitation Jewelry; Coin

SECTION XV: Base Metals and Articles of Base Metals

SECTION XVI: Machinery and Mechanical Appliances; Electrical Equipment; Parts Thereof; Sound Recorders and Reproducers, Television Image and Sound Recorders and Reproducers, and Parts and Accessories of Such Articles

SECTION XVII: Vehicles, Aircraft, Vessels and Associated Transport Equipment

SECTION XVIII: Optical, Photographic, Cinematographic, Measuring, Checking, Precision,
Medical or Surgical Instruments and Apparatus; Clocks and Watches; Musical Instruments; Parts and Accessories Thereof

SECTION XIX: Arms and Ammunition; Parts and Accessories Thereof

SECTION XX: Miscellaneous Manufactured Articles

SECTION XXI: Works of Art, Collectors' Pieces

and Antiques

SECTION XXII: Special Classification
Provisions; Temporary Legislation;

Temporary Modifications
Proclaimed pursuant To Trade Agreements
Legislation; Additional Import Restrictions
Proclaimed Pursuant to Section 22 of the
Agricultural Adjustment Act, As Amended

Prepare your research notes.

Ten International Trade Tips

Did you know that according to the US Customs regulations CFR 111.91(d), a person who is not a broker who intentionally transacts customs business can be imposed a monetary penalty of $10,000 for each transaction or violation.

2. Date of Exportation means the actual date the merchandise finally leaves the country of exportation for the United States.

3. Minimum quantities to be withdrawn from a bonded warehouse in quantities less than an entire bale, cask, box or other package, or, of in bulk in quantities less than 1 ton in weight on entire quantity imported, whichever is smaller.

4. Merchandise shall not remain in a bonded warehouse beyond the 5 years from the date of importation.

5. Powers of attorney issued by a partnership shall be limited to a period not to exceed 2 years from the date of execution.

6. All powers of attorney for individually, corporation, and associations may be granted for an unlimited period.

7. Liquidation means the final computation or ascertainment of the duties (not including vessel repair duties) or drawback acquiring or an entry.

8. Non-commercial importation means merchandise imported for an individual's personal or hausehold use, or a gift but not imported for sale or other commercial purposes.

9. Any record relating to a drawback claim shall be kept until the third anniversary of the date of payment of claim.

10. A consignee who is not the owner or purchaser who appoints the customs borer shall keep a record pertaining to merchandise covered by an informal entry for two years from the date of the informal entry.

International Trade is exchange of capital, goods, and services across international borders or territories. In most countries, it represents a significant share of gross domestic product (GDP).

Industrialization, advanced transportation, globalization, multinational corporations and outsourcing are all having a major impact on the international trade system. Increasing international trade is crucial to the continuance of globalization. Without international trade, nations would be limited to the goods and services produces with their own borders.

Top Traded commodities (Exports) 2010

1. Mineral fuels, Oils, distillation products, etc.

2. Electrical, electronic equipment.

3. Machinery, nuclear reactors, boilers

4. Vehicles, other than railway, tramway.

5. Plastics and all thereof.

[i] www.cbp.gov

www.cctradeimports.com

http://customsbroker.eventbrite.com